TENOR SAX

101 BROADWAY SONGS

T0117642

Note: The keys in this book do not match the other wind instruments.

Available for
FLUTE, CLARINET, ALTO SAX, TENOR SAX, TRUMPET,
HORN, TROMBONE, VIOLIN, VIOLA, CELLO

ISBN 978-1-4950-5249-1

HAL•LEONARD®

For all works contained herein:
Unauthorized copying, arranging, adapting, recording, Internet posting, public performance,
or other distribution of the music in this publication is an infringement of copyright.
Infringers are liable under the law.

Visit Hal Leonard Online at
www.halleonard.com

Contact us:
Hal Leonard
7777 West Bluemound Road
Milwaukee, WI 53213
Email: info@halleonard.com

In Europe, contact:
Hal Leonard Europe Limited
42 Wigmore Street
Marylebone, London, W1U 2RN
Email: info@halleonardeurope.com

In Australia, contact:
Hal Leonard Australia Pty. Ltd.
4 Lentara Court
Cheltenham, Victoria, 3192 Australia
Email: info@halleonard.com.au

CONTENTS

4 All I Ask of You
5 Any Dream Will Do
6 Anything You Can Do
7 As If We Never Said Goodbye
8 As Long as He Needs Me
9 Bali Ha'i
10 Baubles, Bangles and Beads
11 Brotherhood of Man
12 Cabaret
13 Can't Take My Eyes Off of You
14 Circle of Life
15 Climb Ev'ry Mountain
16 Close Every Door
17 Dancing Queen
18 Defying Gravity
20 Do-Re-Mi
21 Do You Hear the People Sing?
22 Don't Cry for Me Argentina
23 Easter Parade
24 Edelweiss
25 Everything's Alright
26 A Foggy Day (In London Town)
28 Friend Like Me
27 Getting to Know You
30 Guys and Dolls
31 Hello, Dolly!
32 Home
34 How Are Things in Glocca Morra
35 I Believe in You
36 I Don't Know How to Love Him
37 I Dreamed a Dream
38 I Got Plenty o' Nuttin'
39 I Whistle a Happy Tune
40 I've Never Been in Love Before
41 If I Loved You
42 If I Were a Bell
43 If I Were a Rich Man
44 The Impossible Dream (The Quest)
45 It Ain't Necessarily So
46 The Lady Is a Tramp
47 The Last Night of the World
48 Let's Call the Whole Thing Off
49 Love Is Here to Stay
50 Love Me or Leave Me
51 Love Walked In
52 Luck Be a Lady
53 Makin' Whoopee!

54 Mame
55 Mamma Mia
56 Matchmaker
57 Maybe
58 Memory
59 The Music of the Night
60 My Favorite Things
61 Nice Work If You Can Get It
62 Oh, What a Beautiful Mornin'
63 Oklahoma
64 Ol' Man River
65 Old Devil Moon
66 On My Own
67 Once in a Lifetime
68 Once in Love with Amy
69 One
70 People Will Say We're in Love
71 The Phantom of the Opera
72 Popular
74 Seasons of Love
76 Send in the Clowns
77 Seventy Six Trombones
78 Shall We Dance?
79 She Loves Me
80 Sherry
81 Some Enchanted Evening
82 Summertime
83 Sunrise, Sunset
84 Superstar
85 The Surrey with the Fringe on Top
86 The Sweetest Sounds
87 There's No Business Like Show Business
88 They All Laughed
89 They Can't Take That Away from Me
90 Think of Me
91 This Is the Moment
92 This Nearly Was Mine
93 Till There Was You
94 Tomorrow
96 Unusual Way
95 Walk Like a Man
98 What I Did for Love
99 What Kind of Fool Am I?
100 Where Is Love?
101 Who Can I Turn To (When Nobody Needs Me)
102 A Whole New World
103 Will You Love Me Tomorrow (Will You Still Love Me Tomorrow)
104 With One Look
105 Written in the Stars
106 You Rule My World
108 You'll Be in My Heart
107 You'll Never Walk Alone
110 You've Got a Friend
112 Younger Than Springtime

ALL I ASK OF YOU

from THE PHANTOM OF THE OPERA

TENOR SAX

Music by ANDREW LLOYD WEBBER
Lyrics by CHARLES HART
Additional Lyrics by RICHARD STILGOE

© Copyright 1986 Andrew Lloyd Webber licensed to The Really Useful Group Ltd.
International Copyright Secured All Rights Reserved

ANY DREAM WILL DO

from JOSEPH AND THE AMAZING TECHNICOLOR® DREAMCOAT

TENOR SAX

Music by ANDREW LLOYD WEBBER
Lyrics by TIM RICE

© Copyright 1969 The Really Useful Group Ltd.
Copyright Renewed
International Copyright Secured All Rights Reserved

ANYTHING YOU CAN DO

from the Stage Production ANNIE GET YOUR GUN

TENOR SAX

Words and Music by
IRVING BERLIN

© Copyright 1946 by Irving Berlin
Copyright Renewed
International Copyright Secured All Rights Reserved

AS IF WE NEVER SAID GOODBYE

from SUNSET BOULEVARD

TENOR SAX

Music by ANDREW LLOYD WEBBER
Lyrics by DON BLACK and CHRISTOPHER HAMPTON,
with contributions by AMY POWERS

© Copyright 1993 Andrew Lloyd Webber licensed to The Really Useful Group Ltd.
International Copyright Secured All Rights Reserved

AS LONG AS HE NEEDS ME

from the Broadway Musical OLIVER!

TENOR SAX

Words and Music by
LIONEL BART

© Copyright 1960 (Renewed) Lakeview Music Co., Ltd., London, England
TRO - Hollis Music, Inc., New York, controls all publication rights for the U.S.A. and Canada
International Copyright Secured
All Rights Reserved Including Public Performance For Profit
Used by Permission

BALI HA'I

from SOUTH PACIFIC

TENOR SAX

Lyrics by OSCAR HAMMERSTEIN II
Music by RICHARD RODGERS

Copyright © 1949 by Richard Rodgers and Oscar Hammerstein II
Copyright Renewed
Williamson Music, a Division of Rodgers & Hammerstein: an Imagem Company, owner of publication and allied rights throughout the world
International Copyright Secured All Rights Reserved

CABARET

from the Musical CABARET

TENOR SAX

Words by FRED EBB
Music by JOHN KANDER

Copyright © 1966, 1967 by Alley Music Corp. and Trio Music Company
Copyright Renewed
All Rights for Trio Music Company Administered by BMG Rights Management (US) LLC
International Copyright Secured All Rights Reserved
Used by Permission

CAN'T TAKE MY EYES OFF OF YOU

featured in JERSEY BOYS

TENOR SAX

Words and Music by BOB CREWE
and BOB GAUDIO

Copyright © 1967 EMI Longitude Music and Seasons Four Music
Copyright Renewed
All Rights on behalf of EMI Longitude Music Administered by Sony/ATV Music Publishing LLC, 424 Church Street, Suite 1200, Nashville, TN 37219
International Copyright Secured All Rights Reserved

CIRCLE OF LIFE

Disney Presents THE LION KING: THE BROADWAY MUSICAL

TENOR SAX

Music by ELTON JOHN
Lyrics by TIM RICE

Moderately, with an African beat

© 1994 Wonderland Music Company, Inc.
All Rights Reserved Used by Permission

CLIMB EV'RY MOUNTAIN

from THE SOUND OF MUSIC

TENOR SAX

Lyrics by OSCAR HAMMERSTEIN II
Music by RICHARD RODGERS

Majestically

Copyright © 1959 by Richard Rodgers and Oscar Hammerstein II
Copyright Renewed
Williamson Music, a Division of Rodgers & Hammerstein: an Imagem Company, owner of publication and allied rights throughout the world
International Copyright Secured All Rights Reserved

CLOSE EVERY DOOR

from JOSEPH AND THE AMAZING TECHNICOLOR® DREAMCOAT

TENOR SAX

Music by ANDREW LLOYD WEBBER
Lyrics by TIM RICE

Moderately, expressively

© Copyright 1969 The Really Useful Group Ltd.
Copyright Renewed
International Copyright Secured All Rights Reserved

DANCING QUEEN

from MAMMA MIA!

TENOR SAX

Words and Music by BENNY ANDERSSON,
BJÖRN ULVAEUS and STIG ANDERSON

Copyright © 1977 UNIVERSAL/UNION SONGS MUSIKFORLAG AB
Copyright Renewed
All Rights in the United States and Canada Controlled and Administered by
UNIVERSAL - SONGS OF POLYGRAM INTERNATIONAL, INC. and EMI GROVE PARK MUSIC, INC.
All Rights Reserved Used by Permission

DEFYING GRAVITY

from the Broadway Musical WICKED

TENOR SAX

Music and Lyrics by
STEPHEN SCHWARTZ

Copyright © 2003 Grey Dog Music
All Rights Reserved Used by Permission

Tempo I

DO-RE-MI

from THE SOUND OF MUSIC

TENOR SAX

Lyrics by OSCAR HAMMERSTEIN II
Music by RICHARD RODGERS

Copyright © 1959 by Richard Rodgers and Oscar Hammerstein II
Copyright Renewed
Williamson Music, a Division of Rodgers & Hammerstein: an Imagem Company, owner of publication and allied rights throughout the world
International Copyright Secured All Rights Reserved

DO YOU HEAR THE PEOPLE SING?

from LES MISÉRABLES

TENOR SAX

Music by CLAUDE-MICHEL SCHÖNBERG
Lyrics by ALAIN BOUBLIL, JEAN-MARC NATEL
and HERBERT KRETZMER

March tempo

Music and French Lyrics Copyright © 1980 by Editions Musicales Alain Boublil
English Lyrics Copyright © 1986 by Alain Boublil Music Ltd. (ASCAP)
Mechanical and Publication Rights for the U.S.A. Administered by Alain Boublil Music Ltd. (ASCAP) c/o Spielman Koenigsberg & Parker LLP,
Richard Koenigsberg, 1745 Broadway, New York NY 10019, Tel 212-453-2500, Fax 212-453-2550, ABML@skpny.com
International Copyright Secured. All Rights Reserved. This music is copyright. Photocopying is illegal.
All Performance Rights Restricted.

DON'T CRY FOR ME ARGENTINA

from EVITA

TENOR SAX

Words by TIM RICE
Music by ANDREW LLOYD WEBBER

Copyright © 1976, 1977 EVITA MUSIC LTD.
Copyright Renewed
All Rights for the United States and Canada Controlled and Administered by UNIVERSAL MUSIC CORP.
All Rights Reserved Used by Permission

EASTER PARADE

from AS THOUSANDS CHEER

TENOR SAX

Words and Music by
IRVING BERLIN

© Copyright 1933 by Irving Berlin
Copyright Renewed
International Copyright Secured All Rights Reserved

EDELWEISS

from THE SOUND OF MUSIC

TENOR SAX

Lyrics by OSCAR HAMMERSTEIN II
Music by RICHARD RODGERS

Slowly, with expression

Copyright © 1959 by Richard Rodgers and Oscar Hammerstein II
Copyright Renewed
Williamson Music, a Division of Rodgers & Hammerstein: an Imagem Company, owner of publication and allied rights throughout the world
International Copyright Secured All Rights Reserved

EVERYTHING'S ALRIGHT

from JESUS CHRIST SUPERSTAR

TENOR SAX

Words by TIM RICE
Music by ANDREW LLOYD WEBBER

Copyright © 1970, 1971 UNIVERSAL / MCA MUSIC LTD.
Copyrights Renewed
All Rights for the U.S. and Canada Controlled and Administered by UNIVERSAL MUSIC CORP.
All Rights Reserved Used by Permission

A FOGGY DAY (IN LONDON TOWN)

from A DAMSEL IN DISTRESS

TENOR SAX

Music and Lyrics by GEORGE GERSHWIN
and IRA GERSHWIN

Moderately

© 1937 (Renewed) NOKAWI MUSIC, FRANKIE G. SONGS and IRA GERSHWIN MUSIC
All Rights for NOKAWI MUSIC Administered by IMAGEM SOUNDS
All Rights for FRANKIE G. SONGS Administered by SONGS MUSIC PUBLISHING
All Rights for IRA GERSHWIN MUSIC Administered by WB MUSIC CORP.
All Rights Reserved Used by Permission

GETTING TO KNOW YOU

from THE KING AND I

TENOR SAX

Lyrics by OSCAR HAMMERSTEIN II
Music by RICHARD RODGERS

Moderately

Copyright © 1951 by Richard Rodgers and Oscar Hammerstein II
Copyright Renewed
Williamson Music, a Division of Rodgers & Hammerstein: an Imagem Company, owner of publication and allied rights throughout the world
International Copyright Secured All Rights Reserved

FRIEND LIKE ME

(Stageplay Version)

from the Walt Disney Stageplay ALADDIN

TENOR SAX

Music by ALAN MENKEN
Lyrics by HOWARD ASHMAN
and STEPHEN SCHWARTZ

© 2014 Walt Disney Music Company and Wonderland Music Company, Inc.
All Rights Reserved Used by Permission

HOME

from Walt Disney's BEAUTY AND THE BEAST: THE BROADWAY MUSICAL

TENOR SAX

Music by ALAN MENKEN
Lyrics by TIM RICE

© 1994 Wonderland Music Company, Inc., Menken Music, Trunksong Music Ltd. and Walt Disney Music Company
All Rights Reserved Used by Permission

1.
2.

HOW ARE THINGS IN GLOCCA MORRA

from FINIAN'S RAINBOW

TENOR SAX

Words by E.Y. "YIP" HARBURG
Music by BURTON LANE

Slowly

Copyright © 1946 by Chappell & Co., Inc. and Glocca Morra Music
Copyright Renewed
All Rights for Glocca Morra Music Administered by Shapiro, Bernstein & Co., Inc., New York
International Copyright Secured All Rights Reserved

I BELIEVE IN YOU

from HOW TO SUCCEED IN BUSINESS WITHOUT REALLY TRYING

TENOR SAX

By FRANK LOESSER

© 1961 (Renewed) FRANK MUSIC CORP.
All Rights Reserved

I DON'T KNOW HOW TO LOVE HIM

from JESUS CHRIST SUPERSTAR

TENOR SAX

Words by TIM RICE
Music by ANDREW LLOYD WEBBER

Slowly, expressively

Copyright © 1971 UNIVERSAL / MCA MUSIC LTD.
Copyright Renewed
All Rights for the U.S. and Canada Controlled and Administered by UNIVERSAL MUSIC CORP.
All Rights Reserved Used by Permission

I DREAMED A DREAM

from LES MISÉRABLES

TENOR SAX

Music by CLAUDE-MICHEL SCHÖNBERG
Lyrics by ALAIN BOUBLIL, JEAN-MARC NATEL
and HERBERT KRETZMER

Moderately slow

Music and French Lyrics Copyright © 1980 by Editions Musicales Alain Boublil
English Lyrics Copyright © 1986 by Alain Boublil Music Ltd. (ASCAP)
Mechanical and Publication Rights for the U.S.A. Administered by Alain Boublil Music Ltd. (ASCAP) c/o Spielman Koenigsberg & Parker LLP,
Richard Koenigsberg, 1745 Broadway, New York NY 10019, Tel 212-453-2500, Fax 212-453-2550, ABML@skpny.com
International Copyright Secured. All Rights Reserved. This music is copyright. Photocopying is illegal.
All Performance Rights Restricted.

I'VE NEVER BEEN IN LOVE BEFORE

from GUYS AND DOLLS

TENOR SAX

By FRANK LOESSER

© 1950 (Renewed) FRANK MUSIC CORP.
All Rights Reserved

IF I LOVED YOU

from CAROUSEL

TENOR SAX

Lyrics by OSCAR HAMMERSTEIN II
Music by RICHARD RODGERS

Copyright © 1945 by Williamson Music, a Division of Rodgers & Hammerstein: an Imagem Company
Copyright Renewed
International Copyright Secured All Rights Reserved

IF I WERE A BELL

from GUYS AND DOLLS

TENOR SAX

By FRANK LOESSER

© 1950 (Renewed) FRANK MUSIC CORP.
All Rights Reserved

IF I WERE A RICH MAN

from the Musical FIDDLER ON THE ROOF

TENOR SAX

Words by SHELDON HARNICK
Music by JERRY BOCK

Copyright © 1964 Bock IP LLC and Mayerling Productions, Ltd.
Copyright Renewed 1992
All Rights for Mayerling Productions, Ltd. Administered by R&H Music, a Division of Rodgers & Hammerstein: an Imagem Company
International Copyright Secured All Rights Reserved

THE IMPOSSIBLE DREAM

(The Quest)

from MAN OF LA MANCHA

TENOR SAX

Lyric by JOE DARION
Music by MITCH LEIGH

Copyright © 1965 (Renewed 1994) Andrew Scott, Inc. and Helena Music Corp.
International Copyright Secured All Rights Reserved

IT AIN'T NECESSARILY SO

from PORGY AND BESS®

TENOR SAX

Music and Lyrics by GEORGE GERSHWIN,
DuBOSE and DOROTHY HEYWARD
and IRA GERSHWIN

© 1935 (Renewed) NOKAWI MUSIC, FRANKIE G. SONGS, DuBOSE AND DOROTHY HEYWARD MEMORIAL FUND PUBLISHING and IRA GERSHWIN MUSIC
All Rights for NOKAWI MUSIC Administered by IMAGEM SOUNDS
All Rights for FRANKIE G. SONGS and DuBOSE AND DOROTHY HEYWARD MEMORIAL FUND PUBLISHING Administered by SONGS MUSIC PUBLISHING
All Rights for IRA GERSHWIN MUSIC Administered by WB MUSIC CORP.
All Rights Reserved Used by Permission

THE LADY IS A TRAMP

from BABES IN ARMS

TENOR SAX

Words by LORENZ HART
Music by RICHARD RODGERS

Copyright © 1937 by Chappell & Co.
Copyright Renewed and Assigned to Imagem CV and WB Music Corp. for the United States and British Reversionary Territories
International Copyright Secured All Rights Reserved

THE LAST NIGHT OF THE WORLD

from MISS SAIGON

TENOR SAX

Music by CLAUDE-MICHEL SCHÖNBERG
Lyrics by ALAIN BOUBLIL and RICHARD MALTBY JR.
Adapted from original French Lyrics by ALAIN BOUBLIL

Languidly

© Copyright (Music and French Lyrics) 1987, © Copyright (English Lyrics) 1988,
© Copyright (Additional Music & English Lyrics) 1989 by Alain Boublil Music Ltd.
Mechanical and Publication Rights for the U.S.A. Administered by Alain Boublil Music Ltd. (ASCAP) c/o Spielman Koenigsberg & Parker LLP,
Richard Koenigsberg, 1745 Broadway, New York NY 10019, Tel 212-453-2500, Fax 212-453-2550, ABML@skpny.com
International Copyright Secured. All Rights Reserved. This music is copyright. Photocopying is illegal.
All Performance Rights Restricted.

LET'S CALL THE WHOLE THING OFF

from SHALL WE DANCE

TENOR SAX

Music and Lyrics by GEORGE GERSHWIN
and IRA GERSHWIN

© 1936 (Renewed) NOKAWI MUSIC, FRANKIE G. SONGS and IRA GERSHWIN MUSIC
All Rights for NOKAWI MUSIC Administered by IMAGEM SOUNDS
All Rights for FRANKIE G. SONGS Administered by SONGS MUSIC PUBLISHING
All Rights for IRA GERSHWIN MUSIC Administered by WB MUSIC CORP.
All Rights Reserved Used by Permission

LOVE IS HERE TO STAY

from GOLDWYN FOLLIES

TENOR SAX

Music and Lyrics by GEORGE GERSHWIN
and IRA GERSHWIN

Medium Swing (♩♫ = ♩♪)

© 1938 (Renewed) NOKAWI MUSIC, FRANKIE G. SONGS and IRA GERSHWIN MUSIC
All Rights for NOKAWI MUSIC Administered by IMAGEM SOUNDS
All Rights for FRANKIE G. SONGS Administered by SONGS MUSIC PUBLISHING
All Rights for IRA GERSHWIN MUSIC Administered by WB MUSIC CORP.
All Rights Reserved Used by Permission

LOVE ME OR LEAVE ME

from WHOOPEE!

TENOR SAX

Lyrics by GUS KAHN
Music by WALTER DONALDSON

Copyright © 1928 (Renewed) by Donaldson Publishing Co., Dreyer Music Co. and Gilbert Keyes Music Co.
All Rights for Dreyer Music Co. Administered by Larry Spier, Inc., New York
All Rights for Gilbert Keyes Music Co. Administered by WB Music Corp.
International Copyright Secured All Rights Reserved

LOVE WALKED IN

from GOLDWYN FOLLIES

TENOR SAX

Music and Lyrics by GEORGE GERSHWIN
and IRA GERSHWIN

Moderately

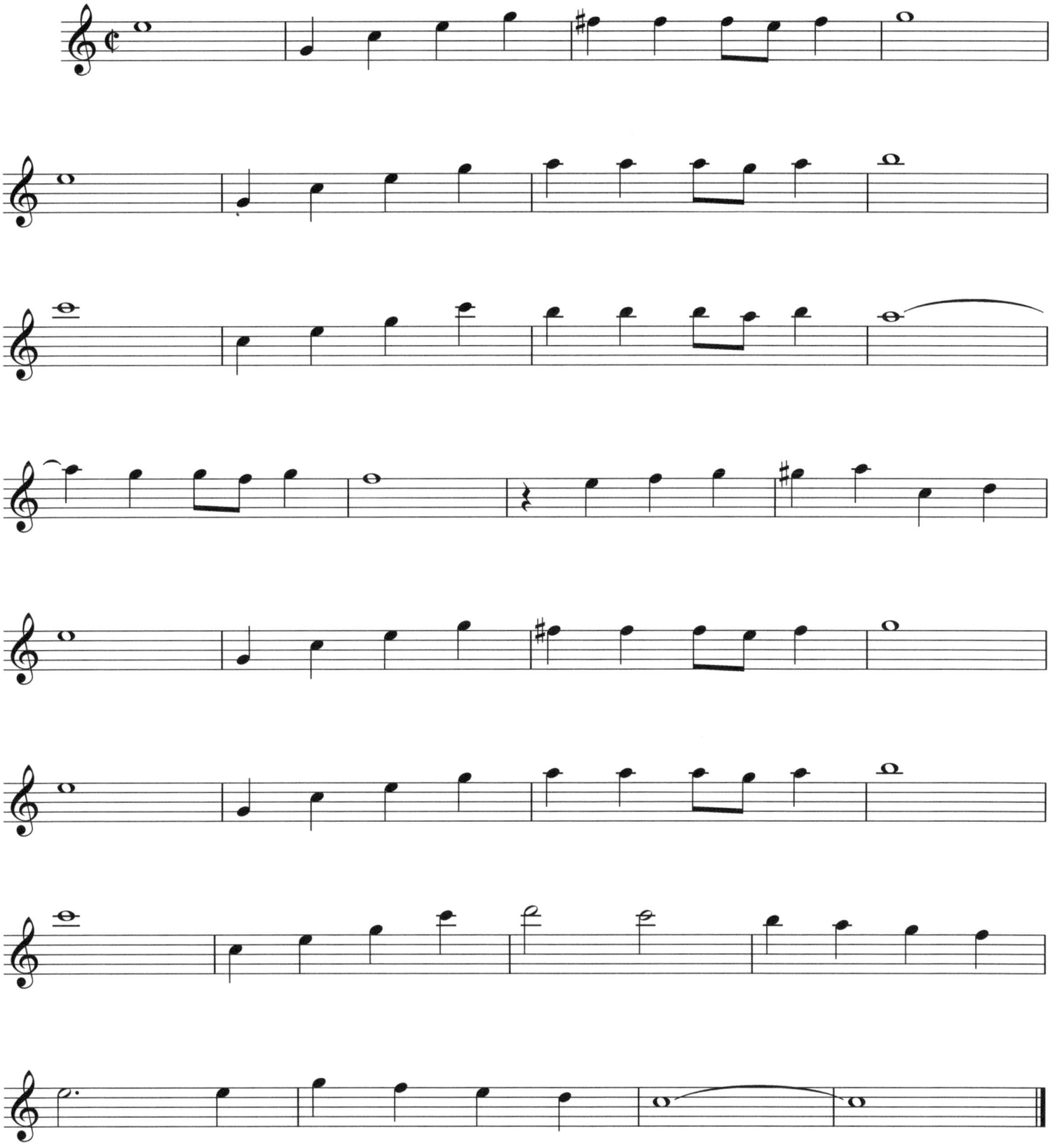

© 1937, 1938 (Copyrights Renewed) NOKAWI MUSIC, FRANKIE G. SONGS and IRA GERSHWIN MUSIC
All Rights for NOKAWI MUSIC Administered by IMAGEM SOUNDS
All Rights for FRANKIE G. SONGS Administered by SONGS MUSIC PUBLISHING
All Rights for IRA GERSHWIN MUSIC Administered by WB MUSIC CORP.
All Rights Reserved Used by Permission

LUCK BE A LADY

from GUYS AND DOLLS

TENOR SAX

By FRANK LOESSER

© 1950 (Renewed) FRANK MUSIC CORP.
All Rights Reserved

MAKIN' WHOOPEE!

from WHOOPEE!

TENOR SAX

Lyrics by GUS KAHN
Music by WALTER DONALDSON

Copyright © 1928 (Renewed) by Donaldson Publishing Co., Dreyer Music Co. and Gilbert Keyes Music Company
All Rights for Dreyer Music Co. Administered by Larry Spier, Inc., New York
All Rights for Gilbert Keyes Music Company Administered by WB Music Corp.
International Copyright Secured All Rights Reserved

MAME

from MAME

TENOR SAX

Music and Lyric by
JERRY HERMAN

© 1966 (Renewed) JERRY HERMAN
All Rights Controlled by JERRYCO MUSIC CO.
Exclusive Agent: EDWIN H. MORRIS & COMPANY, A Division of MPL Music Publishing, Inc.
All Rights Reserved

MAMMA MIA

from MAMMA MIA!

TENOR SAX

Words and Music by BENNY ANDERSSON,
BJÖRN ULVAEUS and STIG ANDERSON

Copyright © 1975 UNIVERSAL/UNION SONGS MUSIKFORLAG AB
Copyright Renewed
All Rights in the United States and Canada Controlled and Administered by
UNIVERSAL - SONGS OF POLYGRAM INTERNATIONAL, INC. and EMI GROVE PARK MUSIC, INC.
Exclusive Print Rights for EMI GROVE PARK MUSIC, INC. Administered by ALFRED MUSIC
All Rights for UK/Eire Administered by BOCU MUSIC LTD.
All Rights Reserved Used by Permission

MATCHMAKER

from the Musical FIDDLER ON THE ROOF

TENOR SAX

Words by SHELDON HARNICK
Music by JERRY BOCK

Copyright © 1964 Bock IP LLC and Mayerling Productions, Ltd.
Copyright Renewed 1992
All Rights for Mayerling Productions, Ltd. Administered by R&H Music, a Division of Rodgers & Hammerstein: an Imagem Company
International Copyright Secured All Rights Reserved

MAYBE

from the Musical Production ANNIE

TENOR SAX

Lyric by MARTIN CHARNIN
Music by CHARLES STROUSE

© 1977 (Renewed) EDWIN H. MORRIS & COMPANY, A Division of MPL Music Publishing, Inc. and CHARLES STROUSE PUBLISHING
All Rights for CHARLES STROUSE PUBLISHING Administered by WB MUSIC CORP.
All Rights Reserved Used by Permission

MEMORY

from CATS

TENOR SAX

Music by ANDREW LLOYD WEBBER
Text by TREVOR NUNN after T.S. ELIOT

Music Copyright © 1981 Andrew Lloyd Webber licensed to The Really Useful Group Ltd.
Text Copyright © 1981 Trevor Nunn and Set Copyrights Ltd.
All Rights in the text Controlled by Faber and Faber Ltd. and Administered for the United States and Canada by
R&H Music Co., a Division of Rodgers & Hammerstein: an Imagem Company
International Copyright Secured All Rights Reserved

THE MUSIC OF THE NIGHT

from THE PHANTOM OF THE OPERA

TENOR SAX

Music by ANDREW LLOYD WEBBER
Lyrics by CHARLES HART
Additional Lyrics by RICHARD STILGOE

Moderately slow

© Copyright 1986 Andrew Lloyd Webber licensed to The Really Useful Group Ltd.
International Copyright Secured All Rights Reserved

MY FAVORITE THINGS

from THE SOUND OF MUSIC

TENOR SAX

Lyrics by OSCAR HAMMERSTEIN II
Music by RICHARD RODGERS

Copyright © 1959 by Richard Rodgers and Oscar Hammerstein II
Copyright Renewed
Williamson Music, a Division of Rodgers & Hammerstein: an Imagem Company, owner of publication and allied rights throughout the world
International Copyright Secured All Rights Reserved

NICE WORK IF YOU CAN GET IT

from A DAMSEL IN DISTRESS

TENOR SAX

Music and Lyrics by GEORGE GERSHWIN
and IRA GERSWIN

© 1937 (Renewed) NOKAWI MUSIC, FRANKIE G. SONGS and IRA GERSHWIN MUSIC
All Rights for NOKAWI MUSIC Administered by IMAGEM SOUNDS
All Rights for FRANKIE G. SONGS Administered by SONGS MUSIC PUBLISHING
All Rights for IRA GERSHWIN MUSIC Administered by WB MUSIC CORP.
All Rights Reserved Used by Permission

OH, WHAT A BEAUTIFUL MORNIN'

from OKLAHOMA!

TENOR SAX

Lyrics by OSCAR HAMMERSTEIN II
Music by RICHARD RODGERS

Bright Waltz

Copyright © 1943 by Williamson Music, a Division of Rodgers & Hammerstein: an Imagem Company
Copyright Renewed
International Copyright Secured All Rights Reserved

OKLAHOMA

from OKLAHOMA!

TENOR SAX

Lyrics by OSCAR HAMMERSTEIN II
Music by RICHARD RODGERS

Copyright © 1943 by Williamson Music, a Division of Rodgers & Hammerstein: an Imagem Company
Copyright Renewed
International Copyright Secured All Rights Reserved

OL' MAN RIVER

from SHOW BOAT

TENOR SAX

Lyrics by OSCAR HAMMERSTEIN II
Music by JEROME KERN

Copyright © 1927 UNIVERSAL - POLYGRAM INTERNATIONAL PUBLISHING, INC.
Copyright Renewed
All Rights Reserved Used by Permission

OLD DEVIL MOON

from FINIAN'S RAINBOW

TENOR SAX

Words by E.Y. "YIP" HARBURG
Music by BURTON LANE

Copyright © 1946 by Chappell & Co., Inc. and Glocca Morra Music
Copyright Renewed
All Rights for Glocca Morra Music Administered by Shapiro, Bernstein & Co., Inc.
International Copyright Secured All Rights Reserved

ON MY OWN

from LES MISÉRABLES

TENOR SAX

Music by CLAUDE-MICHEL SCHÖNBERG
Lyrics by ALAIN BOUBLIL, JEAN-MARC NATEL,
HERBERT KRETZMER, JOHN CAIRD
and TREVOR NUNN

Moderately slow

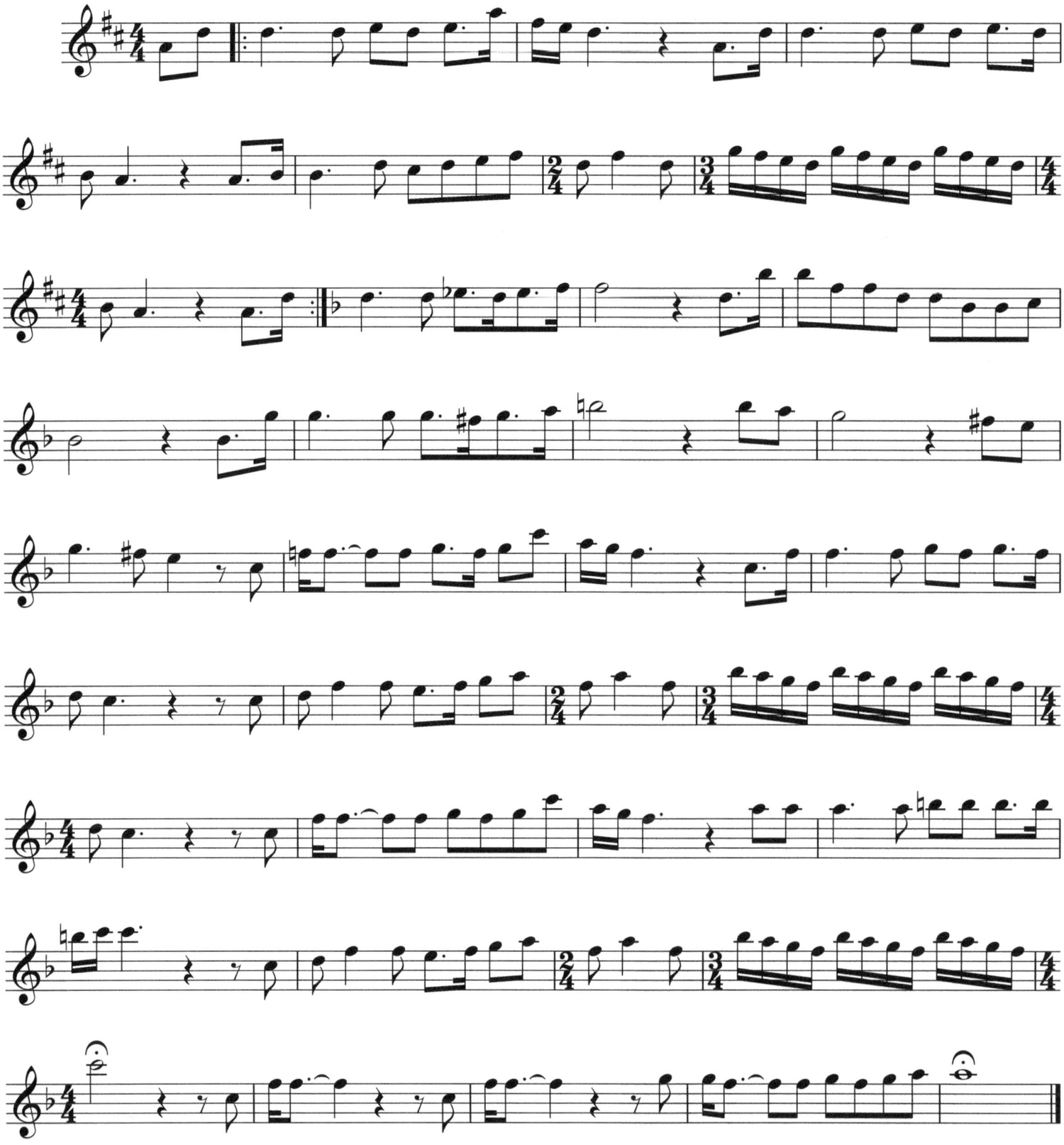

Music and French Lyrics Copyright © 1980 by Editions Musicales Alain Boublil
English Lyrics Copyright © 1986 by Alain Boublil Music Ltd. (ASCAP)
Mechanical and Publication Rights for the U.S.A. Administered by Alain Boublil Music Ltd. (ASCAP) c/o Spielman Koenigsberg & Parker LLP,
Richard Koenigsberg, 1745 Broadway, New York NY 10019, Tel 212-453-2500, Fax 212-453-2550, ABML@skpny.com
International Copyright Secured. All Rights Reserved. This music is copyright. Photocopying is illegal.
All Performance Rights Restricted.

ONCE IN A LIFETIME

from the Musical Production STOP THE WORLD—I WANT TO GET OFF

TENOR SAX

Words and Music by LESLIE BRICUSSE
and ANTHONY NEWLEY

© Copyright 1961 (Renewed) TRO Essex Music Ltd., London, England
TRO - Ludlow Music, Inc., New York, controls all publication rights for the U.S.A. and Canada
International Copyright Secured
All Rights Reserved Including Public Performance For Profit
Used by Permission

ONCE IN LOVE WITH AMY

from WHERE'S CHARLEY?

TENOR SAX

By FRANK LOESSER

© 1948 (Renewed) FRANK MUSIC CORP.
All Rights Reserved

ONE

from A CHORUS LINE

TENOR SAX

Music by MARVIN HAMLISCH
Lyric by EDWARD KLEBAN

© 1975 (Renewed) EDWARD KLEBAN and SONY/ATV MUSIC PUBLISHING LLC
All Rights for EDWARD KLEBAN Controlled by WREN MUSIC CO.
All Rights for SONY/ATV MUSIC PUBLISHING LLC Administered by SONY/ATV MUSIC PUBLISHING LLC, 424 Church Street, Suite 1200, Nashville, TN 37219
All Rights Reserved

PEOPLE WILL SAY WE'RE IN LOVE

from OKLAHOMA!

TENOR SAX

Lyrics by OSCAR HAMMERSTEIN II
Music by RICHARD RODGERS

Copyright © 1943 by Williamson Music, a Division of Rodgers & Hammerstein: an Imagem Company
Copyright Renewed
International Copyright Secured All Rights Reserved

THE PHANTOM OF THE OPERA

from THE PHANTOM OF THE OPERA

TENOR SAX

Music by ANDREW LLOYD WEBBER
Lyrics by CHARLES HART
Additional Lyrics by RICHARD STILGOE
and MIKE BATT

Moderately fast

© Copyright 1986 Andrew Lloyd Webber licensed to The Really Useful Group Ltd.
International Copyright Secured All Rights Reserved

POPULAR

from the Broadway Musical WICKED

TENOR SAX

Music and Lyrics by
STEPHEN SCHWARTZ

Copyright © 2003 Grey Dog Music
All Rights Reserved Used by Permission

SEASONS OF LOVE

from RENT

TENOR SAX

Words and Music by
JONATHAN LARSON

Moderately

Copyright © 1996 FINSTER & LUCY MUSIC LTD. CO.
All Rights Controlled and Administered by UNIVERSAL MUSIC CORP.
All Rights Reserved Used by Permission

SEND IN THE CLOWNS

from the Musical A LITTLE NIGHT MUSIC

TENOR SAX

Words and Music by
STEPHEN SONDHEIM

© 1973 (Renewed) RILTING MUSIC, INC.
All Rights Administered by WB MUSIC CORP.
All Rights Reserved Used by Permission

SEVENTY SIX TROMBONES

from Meredith Willson's THE MUSIC MAN

TENOR SAX

By MEREDITH WILLSON

© 1957 (Renewed) FRANK MUSIC CORP. and MEREDITH WILLSON MUSIC
All Rights Reserved

SHALL WE DANCE?

from THE KING AND I

TENOR SAX

Lyrics by OSCAR HAMMERSTEIN II
Music by RICHARD RODGERS

Copyright © 1951 by Richard Rodgers and Oscar Hammerstein II
Copyright Renewed
Williamson Music, a Division of Rodgers & Hammerstein: an Imagem Company, owner of publication and allied rights throughout the world
International Copyright Secured All Rights Reserved

SHE LOVES ME

from SHE LOVES ME

TENOR SAX

Words by SHELDON HARNICK
Music by JERRY BOCK

Copyright © 1963 Bock IP LLC and Mayerling Productions, Ltd.
Copyright Renewed 1991
All Rights for Mayerling Productions, Ltd. Administered by R&H Music, a Division of Rodgers & Hammerstein: an Imagem Company
International Copyright Secured All Rights Reserved

SHERRY

featured in JERSEY BOYS

TENOR SAX

Words and Music by
BOB GAUDIO

© 1962, 1963 (Renewed) CLARIDGE MUSIC COMPANY, A Division of MPL Music Publishing, Inc.
All Rights Reserved

SOME ENCHANTED EVENING

from SOUTH PACIFIC

TENOR SAX

Lyrics by OSCAR HAMMERSTEIN II
Music by RICHARD RODGERS

Copyright © 1949 by Richard Rodgers and Oscar Hammerstein II
Copyright Renewed
Williamson Music, a Division of Rodgers & Hammerstein: an Imagem Company, owner of publication and allied rights throughout the world
International Copyright Secured All Rights Reserved

SUMMERTIME

from PORGY AND BESS®

TENOR SAX

Music and Lyrics by GEORGE GERSHWIN,
DuBOSE and DOROTHY HEYWARD
and IRA GERSHWIN

© 1935 (Renewed) NOKAWI MUSIC, FRANKIE G. SONGS, DuBOSE AND DOROTHY HEYWARD MEMORIAL FUND PUBLISHING and IRA GERSHWIN MUSIC
All Rights for NOKAWI MUSIC Administered by IMAGEM SOUNDS
All Rights for FRANKIE G. SONGS and DuBOSE AND DOROTHY HEYWARD MEMORIAL FUND PUBLISHING Administered by SONGS MUSIC PUBLISHING
All Rights for IRA GERSHWIN MUSIC Administered by WB MUSIC CORP.
All Rights Reserved Used by Permission

SUNRISE, SUNSET

from the Musical FIDDLER ON THE ROOF

TENOR SAX

Words by SHELDON HARNICK
Music by JERRY BOCK

Moderately slow Waltz

Copyright © 1964 Bock IP LLC and Mayerling Productions, Ltd.
Copyright Renewed 1992
All Rights for Mayerling Productions, Ltd. Administered by R&H Music, a Division of Rodgers & Hammerstein: an Imagem Company
International Copyright Secured All Rights Reserved

SUPERSTAR

from JESUS CHRIST SUPERSTAR

TENOR SAX

Words by TIM RICE
Music by ANDREW LLOYD WEBBER

Copyright © 1969, 1970 UNIVERSAL / MCA MUSIC LTD.
Copyrights Renewed
All Rights for the U.S. and Canada Controlled and Administered by UNIVERSAL MUSIC CORP.
All Rights Reserved Used by Permission

THE SURREY WITH THE FRINGE ON TOP

from OKLAHOMA!

TENOR SAX

Lyrics by OSCAR HAMMERSTEIN II
Music by RICHARD RODGERS

Copyright © 1943 by Williamson Music, a Division of Rodgers & Hammerstein: an Imagem Company
Copyright Renewed
International Copyright Secured All Rights Reserved

THE SWEETEST SOUNDS

from NO STRINGS

TENOR SAX

Lyrics and Music by
RICHARD RODGERS

Copyright © 1962 by Richard Rodgers
Copyright Renewed
Williamson Music, a Division of Rodgers & Hammerstein: an Imagem Company, owner of publication and allied rights throughout the world
International Copyright Secured All Rights Reserved

THERE'S NO BUSINESS LIKE SHOW BUSINESS

from the Stage Production ANNIE GET YOUR GUN

TENOR SAX

Words and Music by
IRVING BERLIN

© Copyright 1946 by Irving Berlin
Copyright Renewed
International Copyright Secured All Rights Reserved

THEY ALL LAUGHED

from SHALL WE DANCE

TENOR SAX

Music and Lyrics by GEORGE GERSHWIN
and IRA GERSHWIN

© 1936 (Renewed) NOKAWI MUSIC, FRANKIE G. SONGS and IRA GERSHWIN MUSIC
All Rights for NOKAWI MUSIC Administered by IMAGEM SOUNDS
All Rights for FRANKIE G. SONGS Administered by SONGS MUSIC PUBLISHING
All Rights for IRA GERSHWIN MUSIC Administered by WB MUSIC CORP.
All Rights Reserved Used by Permission

THEY CAN'T TAKE THAT AWAY FROM ME

from SHALL WE DANCE

TENOR SAX

Music and Lyrics by GEORGE GERSHWIN
and IRA GERSHWIN

© 1936 (Renewed) NOKAWI MUSIC, FRANKIE G. SONGS and IRA GERSHWIN MUSIC
All Rights for NOKAWI MUSIC Administered by IMAGEM SOUNDS
All Rights for FRANKIE G. SONGS Administered by SONGS MUSIC PUBLISHING
All Rights for IRA GERSHWIN MUSIC Administered by WB MUSIC CORP.
All Rights Reserved Used by Permission

THINK OF ME

from THE PHANTOM OF THE OPERA

TENOR SAX

Music by ANDREW LLOYD WEBBER
Lyrics by CHARLES HART
Additional Lyrics by RICHARD STILGOE

© Copyright 1986 Andrew Lloyd Webber licensed to The Really Useful Group Ltd.
International Copyright Secured All Rights Reserved

THIS IS THE MOMENT

from JEKYLL & HYDE

TENOR SAX

Words and Music by LESLIE BRICUSSE
and FRANK WILDHORN

Copyright © 1990, 1995, 1997 Painted Desert Music Corp. on behalf of Stage And Screen Music Inc., BMG Ruby Songs, Scaramanga Music, Inc. and Reservoir Media Music
All Rights for BMG Ruby Songs and Scaramanga Music, Inc. Administered by BMG Rights Management (US) LLC
All Rights for Reservoir Media Music Administered by Reservoir Media Management, Inc.
Reservoir Media Music Administered by Alfred Music
International Copyright Secured All Rights Reserved
Used by Permission

THIS NEARLY WAS MINE

from SOUTH PACIFIC

TENOR SAX

Lyrics by OSCAR HAMMERSTEIN II
Music by RICHARD RODGERS

Copyright © 1949 by Richard Rodgers and Oscar Hammerstein II
Copyright Renewed
Williamson Music, a Division of Rodgers & Hammerstein: an Imagem Company, owner of publication and allied rights throughout the world
International Copyright Secured All Rights Reserved

TILL THERE WAS YOU

from Meredith Willson's THE MUSIC MAN

TENOR SAX

By MEREDITH WILLSON

© 1950, 1957 (Renewed) FRANK MUSIC CORP. and MEREDITH WILLSON MUSIC
All Rights Reserved

TOMORROW

from the Musical Production ANNIE

TENOR SAX

Lyric by MARTIN CHARNIN
Music by CHARLES STROUSE

© 1977 (Renewed) EDWIN H. MORRIS & COMPANY, A Division of MPL Music Publishing, Inc. and CHARLES STROUSE PUBLISHING
All Rights for CHARLES STROUSE PUBLISHING Administered by WB MUSIC CORP.
All Rights Reserved Used by Permission

WALK LIKE A MAN

featured in JERSEY BOYS

TENOR SAX

Words and Music by BOB CREWE
and BOB GAUDIO

© 1963 (Renewed) CLARIDGE MUSIC COMPANY, A Division of MPL Music Publishing, Inc.
All Rights Reserved

UNUSUAL WAY

from NINE

TENOR SAX

Music and Lyrics by
MAURY YESTON

Copyright © 1982 Yeston Music Ltd. (BMI)
All Rights Administered by BMG Rights Management (US) LLC
International Copyright Secured All Rights Reserved

3
3

WHAT I DID FOR LOVE

from A CHORUS LINE

TENOR SAX

Music by MARVIN HAMLISCH
Lyric by EDWARD KLEBAN

© 1975 (Renewed) EDWARD KLEBAN and SONY/ATV MUSIC PUBLISHING LLC
All Rights for EDWARD KLEBAN Controlled by WREN MUSIC CO.
All Rights for SONY/ATV MUSIC PUBLISHING LLC Administered by SONY/ATV MUSIC PUBLISHING LLC, 424 Church Street, Suite 1200, Nashville, TN 37219'
All Rights Reserved

WHAT KIND OF FOOL AM I?

from the Musical Production STOP THE WORLD—I WANT TO GET OFF

TENOR SAX

Words and Music by LESLIE BRICUSSE
and ANTHONY NEWLEY

© Copyright 1961 (Renewed) TRO Essex Music Ltd., London, England
TRO - Ludlow Music, Inc., New York, controls all publication rights for the U.S.A. and Canada
International Copyright Secured
All Rights Reserved Including Public Performance For Profit
Used by Permission

WHERE IS LOVE?

from the Broadway Musical OLIVER!

TENOR SAX

Words and Music by
LIONEL BART

© Copyright 1960 (Renewed), 1968 (Renewed) Lakeview Music Co., Ltd., London, England
TRO - Hollis Music, Inc., New York, controls all publication rights for the U.S.A. and Canada
International Copyright Secured
All Rights Reserved Including Public Performance For Profit
Used by Permission

WHO CAN I TURN TO

(When Nobody Needs Me)

TENOR SAX

from THE ROAR OF THE GREASEPAINT—THE SMELL OF THE CROWD

Words and Music by LESLIE BRICUSSE
and ANTHONY NEWLEY

© Copyright 1964 (Renewed) Concord Music Ltd., London, England
TRO - Musical Comedy Productions, Inc., New York, controls all publication rights for the U.S.A. and Canada
International Copyright Secured
All Rights Reserved Including Public Performance For Profit
Used by Permission

A WHOLE NEW WORLD

from the Walt Disney Stageplay ALADDIN

TENOR SAX

Music by ALAN MENKEN
Lyrics by TIM RICE

© 1992 Wonderland Music Company, Inc. and Walt Disney Music Company
All Rights Reserved Used by Permission

WILL YOU LOVE ME TOMORROW

(Will You Still Love Me Tomorrow)

from BEAUTIFUL

TENOR SAX

Words and Music by GERRY GOFFIN
and CAROLE KING

Copyright © 1961 Screen Gems-EMI Music Inc.
Copyright Renewed
All Rights Administered by Sony/ATV Music Publishing LLC, 424 Church Street, Suite 1200, Nashville, TN 37219
International Copyright Secured All Rights Reserved

WITH ONE LOOK

from SUNSET BOULEVARD

TENOR SAX

Music by ANDREW LLOYD WEBBER
Lyrics by DON BLACK and CHRISTOPHER HAMPTON,
with contributions by AMY POWERS

© Copyright 1993 Andrew Lloyd Webber licensed to The Really Useful Group Ltd.
International Copyright Secured All Rights Reserved

WRITTEN IN THE STARS

from Elton John and Tim Rice's AIDA

TENOR SAX

Music by ELTON JOHN
Lyrics by TIM RICE

© 1999 Wonderland Music Company, Inc., Happenstance Ltd. and Evadon Ltd.
All Rights Reserved Used by Permission

YOU RULE MY WORLD

from THE FULL MONTY

TENOR SAX

Words and Music by
DAVID YAZBEK

Copyright © 2000 Yeidlesounds Co., LLC (BMI)
Worldwide Rights for Yeidlesounds Co., LLC Administered by EMI Blackwood Music Inc.
All Rights Reserved Used by Permission

YOU'LL NEVER WALK ALONE

from CAROUSEL

TENOR SAX

Lyrics by OSCAR HAMMERSTEIN II
Music by RICHARD RODGERS

Copyright © 1945 by Williamson Music, a Division of Rodgers & Hammerstein: an Imagem Company
Copyright Renewed
International Copyright Secured All Rights Reserved

YOU'LL BE IN MY HEART

Disney Presents TARZAN The Broadway Musical

TENOR SAX

Words and Music by
PHIL COLLINS

© 1999 Edgar Rice Burroughs, Inc. and Walt Disney Music Company
All Rights Reserved Used by Permission

D.S. al Coda
CODA
1.
2.
3
3

YOU'VE GOT A FRIEND

from BEAUTIFUL

TENOR SAX

Words and Music by
CAROLE KING

© 1971 (Renewed 1999) COLGEMS-EMI MUSIC INC.
All Rights Reserved International Copyright Secured Used by Permission

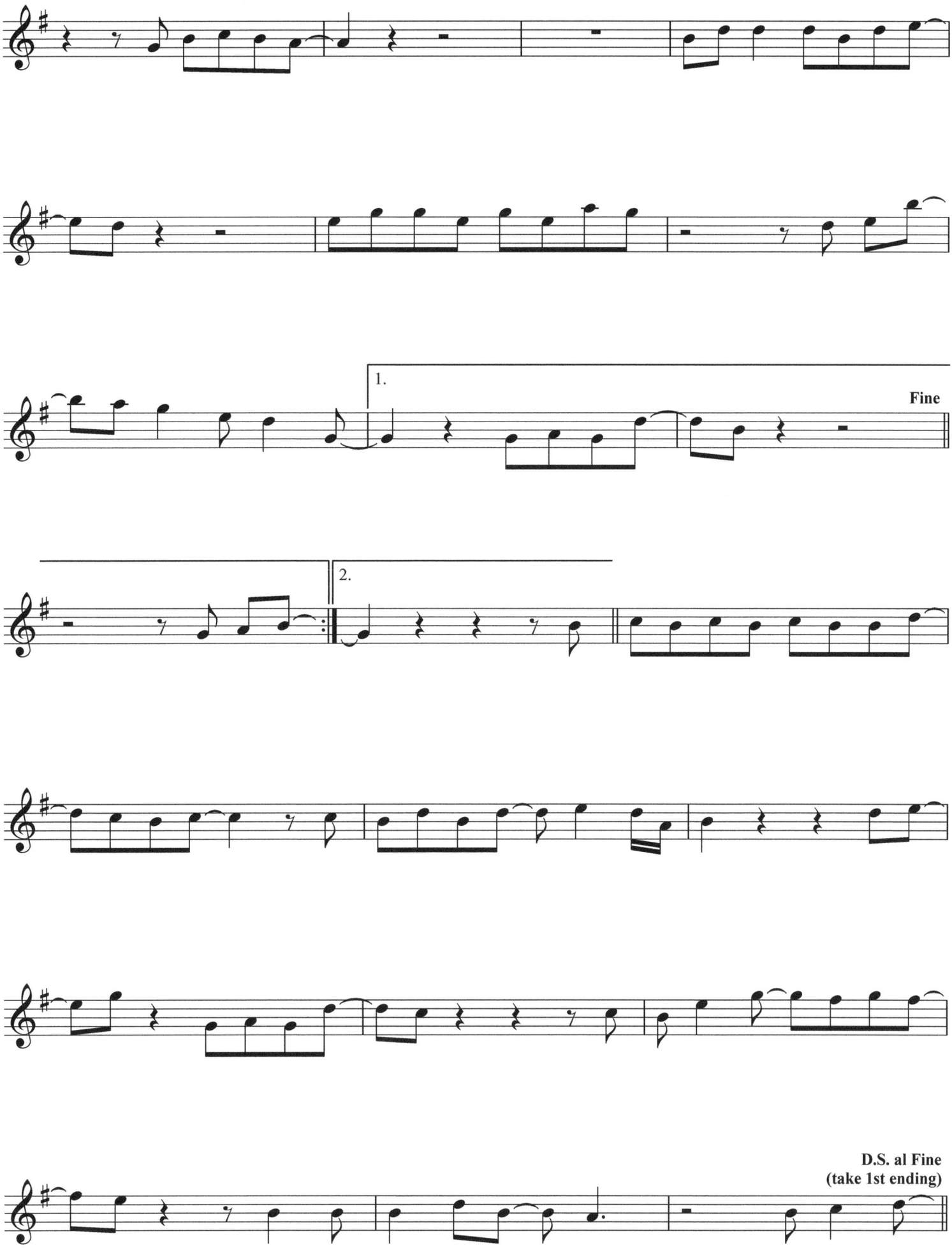
1.
Fine
2.
D.S. al Fine
(take 1st ending)

YOUNGER THAN SPRINGTIME

from SOUTH PACIFIC

TENOR SAX

Lyrics by OSCAR HAMMERSTEIN II
Music by RICHARD RODGERS

Copyright © 1949 by Richard Rodgers and Oscar Hammerstein II
Copyright Renewed
Williamson Music, a Division of Rodgers & Hammerstein: an Imagem Company, owner of publication and allied rights throughout the world
International Copyright Secured All Rights Reserved